AF255223

BEGINNINGS

BEGINNINGS

The First Testament

THIERRY GUILLEMIN

RESOURCE *Publications* · Eugene, Oregon

BEGINNINGS
The First Testament

Resource Publications
An Imprint of Wipf and Stock Publishers
199 W. 8th Ave., Suite 3
Eugene, OR 97401

www.wipfandstock.com

PAPERBACK ISBN: 978-1-6667-7524-2
HARDCOVER ISBN: 978-1-6667-7525-9
EBOOK ISBN: 978-1-6667-7526-6

05/22/23

To God alone be the glory

CONTENTS

CONTENTS

PREFACE

THE POEMS OF THIS collection, for most of them, were written in a strictly contemplative setting, where the continuous reading of the Bible and its meditation was a normal part of daily life. They reflect this meditation as well as the contemplative experience in which they were born, using poetry as a language to go deeper.

The present collection is limited to poems related to texts and the general story narrated in the First Testament, hence the subtitle. They aim to develop a play of natural symbols or others echoing different stories of the Scriptures, up to and including the New Testament. Doing so, they may help deepen the grasp of the biblical text. But they use also for that the unique capacity that has poetry to describe the palette of human feelings and situations. Therefore, they can be read at two basic levels. The first one is natural, with the evocation of emotions and human experiences, like communion with the cosmos, death, mourning, fear, feeling of being broken inside, joy, contemplation, marvel. The second is religious, with the faith content they have. Therefore, anyone can appreciate them without a particular knowledge of the Bible. However, people who are familiar with the Scriptures can go further in the understanding of the poems and hopefully biblical texts at their source.

They were first written in French, and the original text has been placed together with the English translation, as unfortunately the musicality and rhythm at the heart of the French text cannot be conveyed in a translation. But the aesthetic of the images and the strength of the feelings described is fully given in English as in French.

My personal wish, in publishing these poems, would be that they open a door to a personal meditation of the Scriptures.

Finally, I would like to give thanks to everyone who encouraged me, directly or indirectly, first to write these poems, even when I had given up writing, and now to publish them. Without these encouragements and faith, this book would not exist.

Thierry Guillemin

CRÉATION

Du fond de l'abîme émane une lueur aquatique
le chœur des Trois flotte sur l'univers
remplissant le monde d'une voix de silence

La danse des Trois notes devient cosmique
le chaos se fait louange
dans le reflet du temps se célèbrent les noces éternelles
d'un Dieu avec lui-même

Et l'invisible enfante le visible
dans un éclatement de splendeur
la création cachée au secret du Père
surgit hors du mystère
se déployant dans une danse-Dieu à trois voix

Né dans l'alliance éternelle du divin
le monde est image de sa tri-unité

L'amour emporte tout dans son chant souverain
faisant des grains de la matière
les notes de l'hymen qui résonne en elle
et s'en va s'étendre sur la portée du temps

CREATION

From the bottom of the abyss emanates an aquatic glow
the chorus of the Three floats on the universe
filling the world with a voice of silence

The dance of the Three notes becomes cosmic
chaos metamorphoses in praise
in the reflection of time are celebrated
the eternal nuptials
of a God with themself

And the invisible gives birth to the visible
in a burst of splendor
the creation hidden in the secret of the Father
arises out of the mystery
unfolding in a dance-God with three voices

Born in the eternal covenant of the divine
the world is image of their tri-unity

Love carries everything in its sovereign song
making grains of matter
the notes of the hymen that resonates in it
and goes to span the stave of time

LES ANGES

Rayonnement-louange et gardiens de ta gloire
les anges sont là
ils nous entourent

Le regard intérieur vers ta majesté
ils scintillent ta bonté
extasiés dans ton cœur toute une éternité

C'est dans l'incessant cantique de leur *Sanctus*
que les mondes subsistent
nous nous mouvons dans leur adoration

Étincelles du Verbe, flammes de l'Esprit
leur lumière d'amour traverse les espaces
leur chant parcourt l'infini

Tout est tissé de leur prière
tout vibre de leur louange
l'univers est langage de leur vie livrée en grâce
épiphanie du don d'eux-mêmes à ta div-unité

Annonceurs célestes, artisans des volontés divines
ils enflamment les êtres en leur secret
faisant d'eux un encens montant devant ta face
l'âme est illuminée de leur charité

le cœur aride, avide, est embrasé
des tisons ardents de leur contemplation cachée

Témoins de ton mystère
prêtres pour toujours de ta proximité et de ta transcendance
la matière apparaît à leur parole telle une hostie sacrée
la création est la consécration de leur action-de-gloire

Guerriers du premier combat, guides des étoiles
par eux tout n'est qu'eucharistie pétrie d'Esprit
parole de la grâce

Le monde brûle de beauté
corps-mystère où souffle
le silence des esprits

THE ANGELS

Radiance-praise and guardians of your glory
the angels are here
they surround us

The inner gaze towards your majesty
they sparkle your goodness
ecstatic in your heart for an eternity

In the incessant canticle of their *Sanctus*[1]
the worlds remain
we move in their adoration

Sparks of the Word, flames of the Spirit
their light of love crosses the spaces
their song goes through infinity

Everything is woven in their prayer
everything vibrates in their praise
the universe is language of their life delivered in grace
epiphany of the gift of themselves to your div-unity

Celestial announcers, artisans of the divine wills
they inflame beings in their secret
making them an incense rising before your face
the soul is illuminated by their charity

---

1. *Sanctus* means 'holy' in Latin. The verse refers to the song of the angels that the prophet Isaiah heard in his vision of the Lord in majesty (Isaiah 6:3).

the arid, hungry heart is on fire
from the fiery embers of their hidden contemplation

Witnesses to your mystery
priests forever of your closeness and your transcendence
matter appears to their word like a sacred host
creation is the consecration of their glorygiving[2]

Warriors of the first battle, guides of the stars
through them all is but Eucharist imbued with the Spirit
word of grace

The world is burning with beauty
mystery-body where breaths
the silence of the spirits

2. Neologism as in the French text. The word 'Eucharist' (another word to
indicate the Holy Communion) means 'thanksgiving'; the neologism is built
on like the latter word, adapting it to the angelic world.

« QUE SOIT LUMIÈRE ! »

Il n'était qu'un pêlemêle de néant
empli de bruit vide
engourdi de silence
un océan d'absence houleux
en tempête

L'oiselle des origines
flottait sur lui
comme un navire suspendu dans l'air
le couvait
prêt à donner naissance
d'un cri

Du vent de sa bouche
elle modula les mots
et prononça l'espace
où le Père pourrait parler
l'autre-de-Dieu
la Parole triompha du non-dit
et le chaos creva
comme un œuf ouvert

Ainsi surgit
la lumière
du Créateur de sens

Et tout commença

"LET THERE BE LIGHT!"

There was just a jumble of nothingness
filled with empty noise
numb with silence
a choppy ocean of absence
in storm

The she-bird of origins
floated on it
like a ship suspended in the air
brooded over it
ready to give birth
with a cry

From the wind of her mouth
she modulated the words
and pronounced the space
where the Father could talk
the other-of-God
the Word triumphed over the unsaid
and the chaos burst
like an open egg

Thus arises
the light
of the Creator of meaning

And it all started

PREMIERS JOURS

De ses mains de mystère
il saisit l'océan de feu
et le façonna en une immensité de vases de lumière
-tu n'en vois que l'embouchure-

Les anges s'immobilisèrent ébahis
devant les milliers de soleils

Le cri de leur surprise se fixa en notes rondes
et l'émanation du son fit mouvoir les mondes

Alors le chant-Dieu fit danser les lumières

L'univers était nouveau-né
« *Gloire à Dieu au plus haut des cieux !* »
dans la crèche du temps

Et Dieu vit que cela était beau
il fut joie, il fut bonheur

Éternité

FIRST DAYS

From his hands of mystery
he seized the ocean of fire
and fashioned it into an immensity of vessels of light
-you only see the mouth-

The angels stood still amazed
in front of thousands of suns

The cry of their surprise settled in round notes
and the emanation of sound made the worlds move

Then the song-God made the lights dance

The universe was newborn
"Glory to God in the highest!"
in the manger of time

And God saw it was beautiful
there was joy, there was happiness

Eternity

VOIE LACTÉE

Voie lactée
fleuve du souffle divin
s'échappant givré dans le froid d'un hiver sidéral
sillon du mystère où germe la matière
firmament sacré des soleils enflammés de lumière

Le temps tourne sur lui-même comme un manège de séraphins
et l'immense ballet ne s'éteint que dans l'astre de l'aube

Déjà
la lune annonce de sa note joyeuse
la naissance nouvelle de la vie
le chorège du silence
bientôt
rythmera l'instant de son éternité

Bientôt

MILKY WAY

Milky Way
river of divine breath
escaping frosted in the cold of a sidereal winter
furrow of mystery where matter germinates
sacred firmament of suns blazing with light

Time turns on itself like a merry-go-round of seraphim
and the immense ballet is only extinguished in the star of dawn

Already
the moon announces with its joyous note
the new birth of life
the choregos of silence
soon
will punctuate the moment of its eternity

Soon

TROISIÈME JOUR

Le sable d'or coule dans le ciel
voie triomphale où passe le silence
la lumière chante de beauté

Quand soudain
un ange sonne du tonnerre

Le Verbe dit
et le monde fut
la terre surgit des profondeurs
prête à s'habiller de vie

C'est le troisième jour

L'océan, ridé et vaincu, se retire
étirant sa chevelure antique
sur les rives du jour
naissant

Et le grouillement du vivant
commence son épopée
fredonnant un refrain de conquête
illuminant le monde
de son cri de victoire

La germination de l'histoire
s'éveille
dans le bâillement surpris
d'un premier matin

THIRD DAY

Golden sand flows in the sky
triumphal way where the silence passes
the light sings of beauty

When suddenly
an angel sounds thunder

The Word said
and the world was
the earth rises from the depths
ready to dress with life

It's the third day

The ocean, wrinkled and defeated, recedes
stretching its ancient hair
on the shores of the day
nascent

And the swarming of the living
begins its epic journey
humming a song of conquest
illumining the world
with its cry of victory

The germination of history
wakes up
in the surprised yawn
of a first-morning

LES YEUX

Les yeux du Seigneur
toujours ouverts
sur le monde

Le premier
l'œil de jour
traversé de pensées nuageuses
est bleu comme le saphir
y court l'ange de feu
pupille de Dieu

Le second
l'œil de nuit
parsemé des lettres étoilées
tapissant le Livre de Vie
est mystérieux comme le silence
y court l'angelle de clarté
l'autre pupille

Les yeux du Seigneur
toujours ouverts sur le monde
mais l'un après l'autre
quand l'un s'ouvre
l'autre s'éteint
quand l'autre s'illumine

le premier se referme
les yeux du Seigneur

Car toujours l'un regarde le visible
et l'autre l'invisible
en s'alternant
sans fin
regardant
sans répit
les yeux de Dieu

Deux yeux
pour Dieu
révélant son secret
au visible
à l'invisible
révélant son secret
intime
d'altérité

Deux yeux qui s'appellent
en un seul regard
s'effaçant devant le mystère de l'autre
tournant autour de l'éternité
tournant d'amour
en inventant le temps

Les yeux du Seigneur
toujours regardent
le monde
toujours

le Seigneur

pour voir

le pauvre crier vers lui

pour voir

le pécheur

et pleurer sur lui

sa lumière

THE EYES

The eyes of the Lord
always open
on the world

The first
day eye
crossed by cloudy thoughts
is blue like sapphire
there runs the angel of fire
pupil of God

The second
night eye
dotted with star letters
lining the Book of Life
is mysterious like silence
there runs the angelle[3] of clarity
the other pupil

The eyes of the Lord
always open toward the world
but one after the other
when one opens
the other goes out
when the other lights up

3. Neologism like in French, to indicate a 'she-angel' for the moon, in contrast with the 'he-angel' for the sun.

the first closes
the eyes of the Lord

Because always one looks at the visible
and the other the invisible
by alternating
unending
watching
tirelessly
the eyes of God

Two eyes
for God
revealing his secret
to the visible
to the unseen
revealing his secret
intimate
of otherness

Two eyes that call each other
in one look
fading before the mystery of the other
revolving around eternity
turning by love
in inventing time

The eyes of the Lord
always watch
the world
always

the Lord
to see
the poor cry out to him
to see
the sinner
and cry on him
his light

PRIME-JOUR

Au sommet des crêtes de l'océan pierreux
des rafales effilochent l'embrun des neiges
les navires végétaux flottent, immobiles
sur les vagues figées
toute voilure déployée

Leurs mâts, comme des tuyaux d'orgue
laissent s'envoler des mélodies d'oiseaux
les racines du monde chantent
de toutes les rides de leurs troncs

Et, doucement, le silence s'éveille
se retirant devant le rire timide de la forêt
le jour s'apprête à naître en milliers d'ailes en fleurs

Si l'obscurité rôde encor
grognant comme la mort de sa gueule nocturne
la terre halète déjà l'heure en souffles saccadés
déferlant sur les rocs

Les algues aériennes s'étirent
comme des doigts brumeux qui caressent le sol
et les nuages roulent dans le ciel
bientôt tissé de feu

Lorsque soudain paraît

l'œuf

ruisselant de sang

encore incandescent de son enfantement

Le point final est mis à la phrase des nuits

tout s'ouvre de lumière

La première primevère baille en étirant sa blancheur

l'œil écarquillé de surprise autant que de plaisir

le cœur grand ouvert pour embrasser

la vie qui bourdonne près d'elle

Le jour a éclos

comme un bouton de temps

rose d'éternité

PRIME-DAY

Atop the ridges of the stony ocean
gusts fray the snow spray
the vegetal ships float, motionless
on frozen waves
full sails deployed

Their masts, like organ pipes
let the melodies of birds fly away
the roots of the world sing
from all the wrinkles of their trunks

And, slowly, the silence awakens
withdrawing before the timid laughter of the forest
the day is about to be born in thousands of flowering wings

If darkness still lurks
growling like death from its nocturnal maw
the earth is already gasping for the hour in jerky breaths
breaking on the rocks

Aerial algae stretch
like misty fingers caressing the ground
and the clouds roll across the sky
soon woven with fire

When suddenly appears
the egg
dripping with blood
still incandescent from its birth

The full stop is put to the sentence of the nights
everything opens with light

The first primrose yawns stretching its whiteness
eyes wide with surprise as much as pleasure
heart fully open to embrace
the life that buzzes near it

The day has dawned
like a button of time
rose of eternity

LA VIE

La nage poissonne en l'océan
le galop chevale au vent dans un regard qui aigle

La terre arbre son fruit
tandis que la noisette écureuille en grimpant

Montagne, coquelicotte ! Edelweisse-toi, neige !
et toi, bond, vite, chamoise : vois, le sommeil marmotte

Les étangs se nuagent et la pluie se torrente
quand le roucoulement tourterelle de printemps

La fleur se fait abeille et se magie en miel
les prés se vachent blanches en beuglements

Alors que des sauts lapinent un peu plus loin
la ruse se renarde dans un buisson

La marche, elle, fourmit
en queue-leu-leu
à qui mieux mieux

La joie jappe en chien
le jeu chatonne
la peur poule

mais seul l'émerveillement peut se modeler
en un grand cœur d'enfant

La vie
c'est toi, la vie
qui mouvemente en toute chose

LIFE[4]

Swimming fishes in the ocean
gallop horses in the wind in a gaze that eagles

The earth trees its fruit
while the hazel squirrels climbing

Mountain, poppies! Edelweiss yourself, snow!
and you, jump, quickly chamoises: see, the sleep marmots

Ponds cloud themselves and the rain torrents
when the coo doves with spring

The flower becomes a bee and magics into honey
the meadows cow white in bellows

While jumps bunny a little further
cunning foxes itself in a bush

The walk ants
in queue-leu-leu
better to better

Joy yelps in dog
play cats
fear hens

4. The French text is full of neologisms, transforming nouns in verbs for
the meaning of the poem. That has been kept in the English translation.

but wonder can only shape
in a big child's heart

Life
it's you, life
that movements in all things

TES MAINS ONT FAÇONNÉ

Tes mains ont façonné

l'haleine du vent léger et l'herbe qui danse sur la colline

le sang épais de la terre et la couleur de l'eau

la mouche toujours étonnée, l'agile hirondelle jouant avec les cieux

et le regard de l'enfant souriant au regard

Tes mains ont façonné

le saut de l'écureuil affairé et la carpe silencieuse

le soleil qui s'éveille et le lac immobile

la libellule en chasse, le cri du corbeau au loin

et la main de l'enfant tenant une autre main

Tes mains ont façonné

la frêle pâquerette ouverte et le rayon de lune

la baleine blanche sillonnant les mers et le perroquet aux multiples
    couleurs

le cyclone affamé, la plus humble fourmi

et le chant de l'enfant plein de sa joie d'enfant

Tes mains ont façonné

la neige virevoltant et la patience de l'araignée

la gazelle inquiète et l'arbre aux rameaux touffus

le pelage du léopard, l'abeille au miel secret

Et le cœur de l'enfant tout attente d'un cœur

YOUR HANDS HAVE SHAPED

Your hands have shaped
the breath of the light wind and the grass dancing on the hill
the thick blood of the earth and the color of the water
the fly always astonished, the agile swallow playing with the skies
and the gaze of the child smiling at the gaze

Your hands have shaped
the leap of the busy squirrel and the silent carp
the waking sun and the motionless lake
the dragonfly on the hunt, the cry of the crow in the distance
and the child's hand holding another hand

Your hands have shaped
the frail open daisy and the moonbeam
the white whale plying the seas and the multi-colored parrot
the hungry cyclone, the humblest ant
and the song of the child full of their childish joy

Your hands have shaped
the twirling snow and the patience of the spider
the worried gazelle and the tree with thick branches
leopard fur, secret honey bee

and the heart of the child all waiting for a heart

L'ENFANT D'HOMME

La Parole parcourt l'étendue de la nuit
et renaît en soleil au matin
sixième jour

L'Esprit prend poussière en l'homme
la matière se dresse
tournant son front vers l'éternité
la beauté façonne un cœur
le faisant naître
en l'enflammant de toi

Et le grand dialogue
commence
dans le regard d'Adam
brille l'image du Soleil

L'âme animée d'amour
ancrée au tabernacle de ta vie
l'enfant plonge ses deux mains
en ta tendresse
pour puiser l'espérance

L'aurore toujours aux lèvres
il danse la joie en toute liberté
pétrit la vie d'éclats de rire
et soulève l'univers de sa prière

Ta sagesse brille
au centre de son être
en lui
tu trouves tes délices
dans ses yeux étincellent les tiens

L'enfant d'homme
est seul assez fragile
pour exprimer ta plénitude

Son nom est
grâce

THE CHILD OF MAN

The Word roams the expanse of the night
and is reborn in the morning sun
sixth day

The Spirit takes dust in man
matter rises
turning its face towards eternity
beauty shapes a heart
giving birth to it
by igniting it with you

And the great dialogue
begins
in Adam's eyes
shines the image of the Sun

The soul animated by love
anchored in the tabernacle of your life
the child plunges both hands
in your tenderness
to find hope

The dawn always on their lips
the child dances the joy in complete freedom
kneads life with bursts of laughter
and lifts the universe with their prayer

Your wisdom shines
at the center of their being
in them
you find your delights
in their eyes sparkle yours

Only the child of man
is fragile enough
to express your fullness

Its name is
grace

IL RIAIT AUX ÉTOILES

La nuit était couleur étoiles
des taches s'allumaient çà et là sur la toile du silence

Les yeux de l'enfançon écoutait la lumière s'écoulant vers la terre
le Peintre des mondes était poète
et ses mots étaient notes de ciel

Des gouttes de ténèbres ruisselaient encor
joignant à la clarté feutrée une odeur de secret
l'enfançon respirait l'univers

La fraîcheur du temps effleura son visage un instant
le souffle imperceptible qui fait voler le vent
déposant sur son cœur un baiser

La nuit le caressait du bout de ses étoiles
il caressait la nuit de ses doigts étendus
elle le regardait, voilée dans un habit de fête
il la contemplait, bercé par ses lèvres de lune
comme elle, il souriait

Il se perdait au loin dans son âme
saisi par la beauté
sa bouche avidement buvait l'infini
qui s'écoulait en lui en une hymne inaudible

il aspirait l'espace de tout son être
vibrait immobile du Respir invisible

Le temps battait plus lentement

Alors
dans un ravissement de bonheur
en haut de la montagne
sur la pointe du pied
sa droite saisissant un rayon de lune
sa gauche enserrant des cordes de lumière
il joua en riant les notes de la Vie

Et la nuit dévoila son secret dans un éclat de troisième jour

HE LAUGHED WITH THE STARS[5]

The night was stars-color
spots lit up here and there on the canvas of silence

The child's eyes listened to the light flowing towards the earth
the Painter of the worlds was a poet
and his words were notes in the sky

Drops of darkness were still streaming
joining to the hushed clarity an odor of secrecy
the child breathed the universe

The coolness of the air touched their face for a moment
the imperceptible breath that makes the wind fly
placing a kiss on their heart

The night caressed them with the end of her stars
they caressed the night with their outstretched fingers
she looked at them, veiled in a festive dress
they gazed at her, lulled by her moonlike lips
like her, they smiled

They were lost far away in their soul
seized by beauty
their mouth greedily drank the infinite
which flowed through them in an inaudible hymn

5. Although 'night' and 'moon' are neutral in English, they become a 'she'
in the poem.

they aspired the space of their whole being
motionless vibrated with the invisible Breath

Time was beating slower

Then
in a rapture of happiness
at the top of the mountain
on tiptoe
their right hand grabbing a moonbeam
their left embracing strings of light
laughing, they played the notes of Life

And the night revealed her secret in a flash of third day

LE FRUIT

Un fruit pourrit encore au cœur de nos entrailles
nous empoisonnant du meurtrier mensonge
nous faisant périr de sa saveur véreuse
pour nous emprisonner au froid de notre enfer

D'un soupir insipide
en sa source il sape notre vie
assoupissant notre âme d'un sommeil visqueux
aux ventouses de méduse avide

Son rire sinueux, insidieux et cynique
s'infiltre en notre esprit
tissant en son obscurité sa toile ensorcelée

Pieuvre vorace
dont les bras enflammés ont fouettés les flots
les fendant en des larmes d'écume
il nous perce de pieuses pensées
promesses prostituées aux saintes apparences
nous entraînant pour nous étreindre
au fond des griffes de son gouffre

Piqûre de scorpion
il verse son venin en venant distiller ses discours
en nos cœurs tout creusés de désirs discordants
les attirants aux souterrains de ses initiations secrètes

pour les y mieux
croquer

Car le fruit te dévore
jusqu'à te faire crever de vérité

Comme un ver qui couve son cadavre
dans ses ténèbres il te ronge
suintant sa mort au secret de ton sang

Hydre aux mille visages de sirènes
hideuse laideur en sa beauté
maître menteur amoureux de sa propre image
admirée au miroir de ses yeux retournés
il a pris son rien pour son tout

Serpent replié sur sa propre splendeur
enroulement de l'être sur lui-même
il prend pour axe sa propre existence
exaltée au-dessus de tous

Oui
un fruit pourrit encore aux profondeurs de mes entrailles
à me tuer de ta filialité

Mais dans ma vie de misère
dans les veines d'une histoire meurtrie de
toi
ta grâce prend feu
venant brûler ma vétusté en ta bonté

Pécheur encore
mais
sauvé déjà

43

THE FRUIT[6]

A fruit is still rotting in the heart of our entrails
poisoning us with the murderous lie
killing us with his wormy flavor
to imprison us in the cold of our hell

With an insipid sigh
at its source he undermines our life
dozing our soul in a viscous sleep
with suckers of greedy jellyfish

His sinuous, insidious and cynical laughter
seeps into our minds
weaving his bewitched web in his darkness

Ravenous octopus
whose flaming arms whipped the waves
splitting them into tears of foam
he pierces us with pious thoughts
prostituted promises with holy appearances
dragging us to hug us
at the bottom-claws of his abyss

6. Although 'fruit' is neutral in English, it is here personalized in a 'he'.
In the second creation myth at the beginning of the Bible, the first couple introduces sin in human history by eating a forbidden fruit, sealing by this act their refusal of their limitations and difference from God. By refusing their otherness, they alter completely their relationship not only with God, but between them and with all creatures. No space is left for 'the other', who must be dominated or seduced to become an object to manipulate at will.

Scorpion sting
he pours his venom by distilling his speeches
in our hearts all hollowed out with discordant desires
and attract them to the subterranean of his secret initiations
for better crunch
them

Because the fruit devours you
to make you die to the truth

Like a worm brooding over its corpse
in darkness it gnaws you
oozing his death in the secret of your blood

Hydra with a thousand mermaid faces
hideous ugliness in his beauty
master liar in love with his own image
admired in the mirror of his upturned eyes
he confused his nothing with his everything

Serpent writhed around its own splendor
winding of the being on itself
he takes his own existence as his axis
exalted above all

Yes
a fruit still rots in the depths of my entrails
to kill me of your filiality

But in my life of misery
in the veins of a history bruised of
you
your grace catches fire
coming to burn my decay in your goodness

Sinner still
but
saved already

LE MONCEAU DE TERRE

Le dos voûté
saisi d'horreur, sans comprendre
ses mains pendaient pleines de terre
tachées d'un sang qui coulait en lui-même
et n'était plus
ouvrant grande sa gueule
la mangeuse l'avait englouti

Un poids de tristesse lui mura les yeux
un visage, beau, chaud, riant
clair comme un printemps qui fleurit de soleil
surgit en lui
puis un autre, non, le même
livide, glacé
pourquoi ?

Il rouvrit les yeux
et la vit sanglotant doucement
prostrée, embrassant la poussière
les mains languissantes, vidées
c'était son fruit

D'épais nuages voilaient le ciel
le froid les mordait à travers leur toison
et le silence pesait sur eux comme une bête
les glaçait comme un venin

Ses poings se fermèrent
un désir de tuer l'étreignit à son tour
tuer l'autre
son fils
meurtrier de son fils
son fils
son autre fils
et il sut
deux hommes à présent se combattraient en lui
jusqu'à la mort
et chacun avait le visage d'un fils

Il secoua sa tête soudain devenue pâle
et pleura à son tour
tout était comme cassé en lui
fragmenté aux racines

Plus loin
un agneau bêla pour appeler son maître
qui n'était plus
il appela
appela
puis se tut

Tout était fini

Un rayon de jour perça le silence obscur

Ils se levèrent

THE MOUND OF SOIL[7]

The back arched
seized with horror, without understanding
his hands were hanging full of soil
stained with blood that flowed within himself
and was no longer
opening wide its mouth
the eater had devoured it

A weight of sadness walled his eyes
a face, beautiful, warm, laughing
clear as a spring blooming with sunshine
arose in him
then another, no, the same
livid, frozen
why?

He opened his eyes
and saw her sobbing softly
prostrate, embracing the dust
with languid, empty hands
he was her fruit

Thick clouds veiled the sky
the cold bit them through their fleece
and the silence weighed on them like a beast

7. In the biblical narration, the older son of the first couple, Cain, murdered his brother, Abel, who was a shepherd.

froze them like venom

His fists clenched
a desire to kill gripped him in turn
to kill the other
his son
murderer of his son
his son
his other son
and he knew
two men now would fight within him
until death
and each had the face of a son

He shook his suddenly pale head
and wept in his turn
everything was like broken inside him
shattered at the roots

Further
a lamb bleated to call its master
who was no more
it called
called
then went quiet

All was finished

A ray of daylight pierced the dark silence

They got up

LA MORT D'ADAM

Comme gueule béante de bête affamée
un cri de douleur restait ouvert en lui
l'Occident s'éloignait

Ses yeux opacifiés, oublieux du chemin
jetaient encore une faible clarté
vers les monts de la première aurore

L'éclair d'un tonnerre rayait son souvenir
et les ronces du temps effaçaient tout
le pays du Verger . . .

Une bruine salée sourdit de ses entrailles
les larmes de sa peur se faufilèrent
à travers la sueur de son corps tiède
et gouttèrent sur le sol

Il faisait froid

L'arbre alors debout venait de se coucher
sa plaie impalpable geignait en silence
mais la blessure hurlait au fond de son âme

À présent
il
connaissait

La saveur ténébreuse du fruit éblouissant
avait mêlé son poison métallique
à son sang
dans les fleuves de vie serpentait désormais
un ruisseau de mort

Il faisait froid

L'obscurité reniflait
les dernières senteurs de son existence
s'évanouissant
et telles des pleureuses
des lambeaux de ténèbres l'entouraient déjà

Dans une hémorragie de feu, le soleil se mourait

Il faisait froid

Il tâta de ses mains la terre humidifiée
qui buvait avidement le flux de sa souffrance
elle demeurait marquée d'une tache rougeâtre

Caïn fuyait toujours dans les monts de Séir

Le soleil n'était plus
il faisait froid
froid

Seule Ève se tenait près de lui

Froid

« Mon Dieu, mon Dieu
pourquoi t'avoir abandonné ?
Je ne savais pas ce que je connaissais. »

Ses deux mains s'étendirent en forme de croix

Comme le scarabée sous les pas d'un passant
il était
écrasé

Froid

Les crimes de ses fils étaient clous dans sa chair
son cœur en agonie suintait la mort
et dans ses os, dansait un brasier
sarabande d'un feu livide consumant sa vie du désir insensé
entraînant son âme en un grand rire vide
mais était-ce le sien

En écho
il jeta
dans un grand
 CRI
son dernier souffle aux étoiles
les bras dressés

Sur ton crâne
Adam
germa un germe d'arbre
l'amour vainquit la mort
et la mort fut pendu

ADAM'S DEATH

Like the gaping jaws of a hungry beast
a cry of pain remained open in him
the West was moving away[8]

His clouded eyes, forgetful of the way
still casted a faint light
towards the mountains of the prime dawn

The lightening of a thunder scratched his memory
and the brambles of time erased everything
the land of Eden . . .

A salty drizzle welled up from his entrails
the tears from his fear threaded their way
among the sweat of his body hardly warm
and dripped on the ground

It was cold

The tree then standing was now lying down
his impalpable wound moaned silently
but the gash screamed deep in his soul

8. In the biblical symbology, Adam and Eve go to East after they have to
leave Eden; therefore, the latter is at the West of where they are.

Now
he
knew

The dark flavor of the dazzling fruit
had mixed its metallic poison
to his blood
in the rivers of life now meandered
a stream of death

It was cold

Darkness sniffed
the last scents of his existence
fainting
and like mourners
shreds of darkness already surrounded him

In a hemorrhage of fire the sun was dying

It was cold

He felt with his hands the moistened earth
who greedily drank the stream of his suffering
it remained marked with a reddish stain

Cain was still fleeing in the mountains of Seir

The sun was gone
it was cold
cold

Only Eve stood by him

Cold

"My God, my God
why did I leave you?
I didn't understand what I knew."

His two hands stretched out in the shape of a cross

Like the beetle under the footsteps of a passerby
he was
crushed

Cold

The crimes of his sons were like nails in his flesh
his heart in agony oozed death
and in his bones danced a brazier
saraband of a livid fire consuming his life of the senseless desire
dragging his soul into a great empty laughter
but was it his

In echo
he threw
in a big
SHOUT
his last breath to the stars
arms raised

On your skull
Adam
sprouted a tree sprout
love conquered death
and death was hung

ALLIANCE

La chaleur de la terre s'élève à effleurer les nuages
volutes invisibles d'encens chargées d'un parfum fleuri

Passe le souffle
et les arbres chantent de toutes leurs feuilles
leurs doigts tendus vers la beauté d'une patrie encore cachée
ces geysers végétaux surgissent d'entre les rochers
puis s'élancent dans l'espace et éclatent en gouttelettes feuillées
index dressés pour toi
témoins et gardiens de ton chemin d'éternité

Écoute le silence du ciel reposer sur la cime des monts
la musique des étoiles s'écouler tremblante de bonheur
c'est la voix des anges s'épanchant en ton cœur

Regarde ruisseler le fleuve de vie
jaillissant du côté ouvert de la Nouvelle Arche
il repeuple le monde
pendant que tu offres au ciel, en tes paumes
Noé
l'hymne de l'univers

Se vidant de tout
elles aspirent l'Infini en leur centre
comme en un puits d'éternité
soudant ciel et terre en lui

Et Dieu déposa sur l'horizon
l'arc aux sept mélodies
devenant vulnérable
aux flèches de nos mots
lancés à sa merci

La coupe de tes bras en prière
s'emplirent de miséricorde
l'alliance était scellée dans une noce invisible

Aube d'un nouveau jour

COVENANT[9]

The heat of the earth rises to touch the clouds
invisible swirls of incense loaded with a floral fragrance

Passes the breath
and the trees sing with all their leaves
their fingers stretched out towards the beauty of a homeland, still
    hidden
these vegetable geysers arise from between the rocks
then soar into space and burst into leafy droplets
indexes drawn up for you
witnesses and guardians of your eternity path

Listen to the silence of the sky resting on the tops of the mountains
to the music of the stars flowing down trembling with happiness
it's the voice of angels pouring out in your heart

Watch the river of life flow
springing from the open side of the New Ark
it repopulates the world
while you offer to the sky, in your palms
Noah

---

9. In the biblical story, humanity reaches such a point of evilness, that every-thing is led toward its destruction. To preserve a remnant before it is too late, God anticipates the end of everything with a Great Flood and saves the last righteous man, Noah, by asking him to build a ship-ark. This ship will serve as a refuge for his family and a couple of each species of animals that will have to repopulate the earth after the flood. After the waters recede and Noah leaves the ark, God passes a covenant of peace with their creatures, giving the rainbow as a sign of it.

the anthem of the universe

Emptying themselves of everything
they aspire the Infinite in their center
as in a well of eternity
uniting heaven and earth in it

And God laid on the horizon
the seven melodies rainbow
becoming vulnerable
to the arrows of our words
thrown at their pity

The cup of your arms in prayer
was filling with mercy
the covenant was sealed in an invisible wedding

Dawn of a new day

LA TOUR

la tour se dressait sur l'horizon
comme un doigt
pointant vers l'Eternel
d'un geste accusateur

l'accomplissement de l'humain
devenait suffisance de lui-même
preuve de sa grandeur inégalée
inégalable
contre celle de Dieu
signe de sa puissance contre Son silence

où était-Il ?
où le Créateur devant Sa non-création
s'élevant en splendeur ?

la tour était grandiose
et la tour était nôtre
la tour était géante
totalement nôtre

elle se dressait, immense
comme une montagne prête à gravir les cieux
les touchant
pour les repousser
à jamais

de l'œuf du pouvoir
créant l'unité d'oppression
devait surgir la gloire
il ne s'en craqua que divisions et guerres
à mort

sur une autre montagne
les cieux touchèrent la terre
pour la caresser de Sa miséricorde
pour l'unir en chant d'action-de-grâce
toute une éternité

THE TOWER [10]

the tower stood on the horizon
like a finger
pointing to the Eternal
in an accusatory gesture

the human accomplishment
was becoming self-important
proof of its unequaled greatness
incomparable
against that of God
sign of their power against Their silence

where were They?
where the Creator facing Their non-creation
rising in splendor?

the tower was grand
and the tower was ours
the tower was huge
totally ours

10. Only what relates to God is endowed with a capital letter. The biblical story of the tower of Babel narrates the rise of the first empire and resurgence of revolt against God; the latter ends it by dispersing peoples who will then adopt different languages: God brings again difference where there was only uniformity, to develop the respect of alterity as the only ground on which love and harmony can flourish. This plan of salvation will find its achievement when all nations will be brought into one church, in the respect of their cultural differences.

it rose, immense
like a mountain ready to climb the skies
touching them
to push them away
forever

from the egg of power
creating unity by oppression
glory was to arise
only cracked from it divisions and wars
to death

on another mountain
heavens touched the world
to caress it with Their mercy
to unite it in song of thanksgiving
for an eternity

LA PROMESSE

Abraham était vieux

Le front de son âme retourné vers le ciel, il contemplait l'Éternel
au-delà de la nuit ; c'était un soir de noce : des milliers de mil-
liers la couvrait de joyaux
En son centre était le plus précieux, serti d'un halo de clarté pâle
et brune
Demain serait beau jour

Abraham était vieux

Abraham regardait plus loin que le regard : ses yeux transperçaient
ce que l'œil ne peut voir
La musique du ciel résonnait en son âme comme un écho craintif
qui dans le silence emplissait tout l'espace

Abraham était vieux

Abraham était seul, seul devant l'Éternel ; les paumes de ses mains
se tournaient et creusaient, prêtes à recevoir le poids d'une
bénédiction divine, ses deux bras se tendaient en un geste
d'offrande, tout son corps était coupe appelant de son désir le
vin nouveau du Royaume
Dans la montagne, là-haut, entre Aï et Béthel, on devinait un arbre
autrefois dressé, mais qui aujourd'hui se courbait

Abraham était vieux

Abraham priait, les rides et le regard tournés vers les vastes éten-
dues profondes, le cœur élevé vers les terres plus grandes de
l'unique Verger ; ses lèvres remuaient laissant ruisseler un
chuchotement paisible, des pensées pétillaient en ses yeux
jouant avec le reflet des milliers de milliers

Plus loin, dans la vallée, se profilait la tache de sa tente ; Sarah le
regardait

Abraham était vieux

Abraham attendait, d'une attente frémissante bridée par la patience
du temps qui se résigne à ne devoir qu'attendre maintenant

« Mon Dieu, mon Dieu, la promesse . . . »

L'interrogation s'éteignit contre un mur invisible, le silence se taisait

Abraham était vieux

Abraham écoutait, ses yeux mi-clos : des profondeurs de sa mé-
moire montait une parole qui revenait sans cesse, vague se suc-
cédant infiniment à elle-même et venant vivre sur la grève des
souvenirs

« Lève les yeux au ciel et compte les étoiles si tu peux les compter :
ta descendance sera telle »

Abraham était vieux

Abraham songeait, il pensait à Sarah demeurée près des feux, et le
souffle de son cœur alla se poser sur son front

« Lève les yeux au ciel »

Dans l'instant d'une image, leurs prunelles s'unirent ; l'éclat des
yeux de leur jeunesse s'était mué en paisible chaleur de braise
du temps des crépuscules

« Et compte les étoiles si tu peux les compter »

Son sein s'était blanchi

Abraham était vieux

La chaîne des âges qui reliait son corps à ce sol argileux perdait
    chaque saison un peu de ses maillons
« Ta descendance sera telle »

Abraham était vieux

Mais Abraham comptait, envahi de plaisir
Il regardait à droite, à gauche, revenait au centre, puis se tournait
    derrière, au-dessus de lui, de nouveau à droite, et à gauche
« Des milliers de milliers »
Et les étoiles semblaient se joindre en une farandole suspendue
    hors du temps, dont leur propre lumière en était la musique

« Abraham, Abraham, lève les yeux au ciel et compte les étoiles si
    tu peux les compter ; compte-les, compte-les : elle sera telle, ta
    descendance »

Sarah était bien vieille et lui bien trop âgé
Mais tant que dans le ciel brilleraient les étoiles,
la promesse vie-vraie

Dans le regard du patriarche, naquit
un rire

THE PROMISE[11]

Abraham was old

The brow of his soul turned towards heavens, he contemplated the
    Eternal beyond the night; it was a wedding night: thousands of
    thousands covered it with jewels
In its center was the most precious, set in a halo of pale, brown clarity
Tomorrow would be a good day

Abraham was old

Abraham looked beyond the gaze: his eyes pierced what the eye
    cannot see
The music of the sky resounded in his soul like a timid echo which
    in the silence filled all the space

Abraham was old

Abraham was alone, alone before the Eternal; the palms of his
    hands turned and hollowed, ready to receive the weight of a
    divine blessing, his two arms stretched out in a gesture of offer-
    ing, his whole body was cup, by his desire calling for the new
    wine of the Kingdom
In the mountain, up there, between Ai and Bethel, was guessed a
    tree once erect, but that was now bending

11. As evilness prospers again, God uses a new strategy: they will start
again their creation, but not by destroying everything like they did with the
Great Flood; instead, they will transform the world starting again with a
couple. Thus, they reveal themself to a married man, who they promise will
become the father of a descendance as numerous as the stars in the sky.

Abraham was old

Abraham prayed, his wrinkles and his gaze turned towards the
    deep vast expanses, his heart lifted towards the greater lands
    of the unique Orchard; his lips were moving to let a peaceful
    whisper trickling, thoughts sparkled in his eyes playing with
    the reflection of the thousands of thousands
Farther, down the valley, loomed the spot of his tent; Sarah looked
    at him

Abraham was old

Abraham waited, with a quivering expectation bridled by the pa-
    tience of time that resigns itself to having to still wait only now
"My God, my God, the promise . . ."
The question died out against an invisible wall, the silence kept quiet

Abraham was old

Abraham listened, his eyes half-closed: from the depths of his mem-
    ory rose a word that kept coming back, a wave that infinitely
    followed itself and came to live on the beach of remembrances
"Raise your eyes to the sky and count the stars if you can count
    them: your offspring will be such"

Abraham was old

Abraham was thinking, he was thinking of Sarah who had re-
    mained near the fires, and the breath of his heart went to rest
    on her forehead
"Look up to the sky"

In the instant of an image, their pupils united; the sparkle in the
    eyes of their youth had turned into the peaceful ember heat of
    twilight time
"And count the stars if you can count them"
Her womb had become white

Abraham was old

The chain of ages that linked his body to this clay soil lost a few of
    its links each season
"Your offspring will be such"

Abraham was old

But Abraham counted, overwhelmed with pleasure
He looked to the right, to the left, back to the center, then turned
    behind, above him, again to the right, and to the left
"Thousands of thousands"
And the stars seemed to join in a farandole suspended out of time,
    of which their own light was the music

"Abraham, Abraham, raise your eyes to the sky and count the stars
    if you can count them; count them, count them: it will be such,
    your offspring"

Sarah was overaged and he was way too old; but as long as in the
    sky the stars would shine, the promise would live in truth[12]

12. There is a play on the sounds of words in French that cannot be trans-
lated in English. Literally, the verse is 'the promise life-true' because the two
words 'Life' and 'True' put together have the same sound in French than the
verbal group 'would live'.

In the gaze of the patriarch, was born
a laugh[13]

73

13. Isaac means 'the one who laughs' in Hebrew.

SODOME

la fumée
des violent désirs
montait encore du sol
tiède

le feu
crépitant ses projets de crimes
enfer-nait les pensées
ravageait l'esprit
de meurtres muets
qui éclataient en cris crevant l'espace
comme des couteaux

la peur était partout
et partout la misère

la compassion, était meurtrie
blessée de mort cruelle
blessée de mort en croix

l'humanité se rongeait de folie
comme rat aveuglé par sa faim
la limite de l'insanité était
de n'en avoir aucune

la vérité était holocaustée
ensevelie
au tombeau de mensonge

et la vie fut détruite dans l'incendie
qui brûlait aux cœurs
et encendrait Sa vie

tout devait disparaître
tout
pour devenir cendre-humus
sur lequel fleurirait
le nouveau germe

plus loin
sans mouvoir
cadavre engouffré de regret
navire de nostalgie sur la mer de mort
une statue de sel s'était retournée
son regard emmuré en elle

SODOM

the smoke of
violent desires
was still rising from the ground
lukewarm

the fire
crackling its plans of crimes
was locking up the thoughts in hell[14]
ravaging the mind
with silent murders
bursting into cries that slashed the space
like knives

fear was everywhere
and everywhere misery

compassion was bruised
cruelly wounded
mortally wounded on a cross

humanity was consumed with madness
like a rat blinded by its hunger
the limit of insanity was
no limit to have

14. There a play of words in French impossible to translate in English: the verbal group 'locked up' has about the same sound than the words 'hell-born' put together. Literally, the verse in French is: "hell-born the thoughts."

truth was holocausted[15]
buried
in a tomb of lies

and life was destroyed in the fire
that burned in the hearts
and cremated[16] Their life

everything had to go
everything
to become ash-humus
on which would bloom
the new germ

further away
without moving
corpse engulfed in regret
ship of nostalgia on the sea of death
a pillar of salt had turned over
its gaze walled up in it

15. Neologism, like in the French text.
16. Literally, it should be translated by the neologism 'ashed' to keep the French neologism.

L'ÉPREUVE

Père et fils gravissaient ensemble
muets
le mont de douleurs
l'agneau n'était pas là
la réponse du père gisait dans son silence

Au sommet
pierre après pierre, l'autel fut érigé
monument de stupeur
comme un œil figé fixant le ciel
mendiant le sens
espérant l'impossible

Mais rien ne pouvait effacer l'effroyable
requête
le sacrifice qui tuerait
et la victime et le prêtre

Lentement le fils monta
élevé de terre
son regard s'engloutit dans celui de son père

La lame du couteau se dressa
point d'exclamation
prêt à déchirer l'invisible

Un lancinant silence de souffrance
enveloppait tout
le temps semblait suspendu dans l'abîme
chaos des origines

Quand le couteau
s'abattit

Retenu par un ange

L'épreuve était finie

Jour un d'un nouveau peuple

THE ORDEAL [17]

Father and son were climbing together
numb
the mountain of distress
the lamb was not there
the father's answer was in his silence

At the top
stone by stone, the altar was erected
stupor monument
like a frozen eye staring at the sky
begging for meaning
hoping for the impossible

But nothing could erase the dreadful
query
the sacrifice that would kill
the victim and the priest

17. When Isaac is old enough, God formulates a request to Abraham, but us-
ing words having a double meaning in Hebrew: to climb with Isaac on a moun-
tain indicated to offer a sacrifice (and teach to his son the virtue of religion), or
to offer Isaac in sacrifice on a mountain indicated. Abraham understands the
request with the second meaning according to the culture of his time and use
of the surrounding worshipers of idols. God will stop him in his act at the last
seconds, teaching at the same time the value of offering to Them everything
when asked, and that They are different from idols, giving life, not taking it.

Slowly the son ascended
raised from the ground
his gaze sunk into his father's

The blade of the knife stood up
exclamation point
ready to rip the invisible

A haunting silence of suffering
enveloped everything
time seemed suspended in the abyss
chaos of origins

When the knife
fell

Held back by an angel

The ordeal was over

Day one of a new people

LE COMBAT AVEC L'ANGE

La bataille était épuisante

L'échelle
l'avait conduit aux portes du céleste
prière accomplie portée par l'ange
annonçant le fruit du futur

L'ange aujourd'hui s'était dressé
pour barrer le futur
comme un Eden interdit

Jacob affrontait le mystère
la question du 'qui'
lancinante en l'homme
lancinante en lui

Son combat était celui des doutes
comme des mains tâtonnant l'invisible
des questions en quête de réponses
impossibles à comprendre

Seulement dans la blessure du vulnérable
dans la faiblesse confessée
reconnue en attente de guérison
la concession de la limite
gisait la fin du combat

La victoire était dans la défaite acceptée
abandonnement aux mains du Messager d'Aurore
qui renouvelle tout
83

Et l'ange
disparut

THE WRESTLING WITH THE ANGEL[18]

The battle was exhausting

The ladder
had led him to the gates of heaven
fulfilled prayer carried by the angel
announcing the fruit of the future

The angel today had risen
to block the future
like a forbidden Eden

Jacob was fighting the mystery
the question of 'who'
throbbing in humanity
throbbing in him

His wrestle was one of doubts
like hands groping the invisible
questions in search of answers
impossible to understand

Only in the wound of the vulnerable
in the confessed weakness

18. In the biblical narrative, the patriarch Jacob had two important mystical experiences in his life: in the first, he sees a ladder leading to heaven, with angels climbing it and descending it as mediators between human beings and God; in the second, he wrestles with an angel before being blessed.

recognized as awaiting a healing
the concession of the limit
lays the end of the fight

Victory was in defeat accepted
surrender in the hands of the Dawn Messenger
who renews everything

And the angel
disappeared

LA TUNIQUE

Ils étaient là, debout, perdus
leur passé affamé dévorant le futur

La tunique aux multiples couleurs
comme un arc-en-ciel de beauté
brûlait encore en leurs cœurs
tachés
criait encore d'une voix assourdie
assourdissante
'justice'
La tunique aux couleurs de sang

La tunique hantait encore leurs nuits
visitant leurs songes de ses cris quêtant pitié
de ses yeux débordants de larmes
la tunique de sang

La tunique gisait encore vivante
dans la citerne de mémoire
recouverte de lambeaux de distractions
pour oublier
qu'ils ne pouvaient oublier
la tunique

Vendue
esclave du mensonge
prisonnière des caprices interdits
violant l'intégrité

Quand la tunique chanta miséricorde
anticipant le temps
lavant le sang
dans le Sang
l'agneau pascal du déjà sauveur

Une vie nouvelle
commençait
dans un nouveau royaume

La main meurtrie tendue
offrait un futur d'éternité
renée

C'était à eux de l'accueillir
dans un cœur vidé de son fiel
et creusé de confiance

Comme c'est à toi

Quelle est ta tunique de sang ?

THE COAT[19]

They were standing, lost
their hungry past devouring the future

The multi-colored coat
like a rainbow of beauty
still burned in their hearts
stained
was still shouting in a muffled voice
deafening
'justice'
the blood-colored coat

The coat still haunted their nights
visiting their dreams with its cries begging for pity
with its eyes overflowing with tears
the blood coat

The coat still lays alive
in the cistern of memory
covered by shreds of distractions

19. The brothers of Joseph, jealous of him, sold him to traders as a slave and soiled his coat in the blood of an animal to make his father, Jacob, believe that he was killed by a wild animal. But God blessed Joseph who became in fact the vizir of Egypt. Later, during a famine, the brothers go to Egypt and meet the vizir without recognising their brother. After testing them and being assured that they repented of their crime and changed, Joseph reveals to them his true identity and forgives them.

to forget
that they couldn't forget
the coat

Sold
slave to lies
prisoner of forbidden whims
raping integrity

When the coat sang mercy
anticipating time
washing away the blood
in the Blood
the paschal lamb was already savior

A new life could
start
in a new kingdom

The bruised hand outstretched
offered a future of eternity
born again

It was up to them to welcome it
in a heart emptied of its gall
and deepened by trust

It is up to you

What is your blood coat?

LE NOM

Le Nom
brûlait le buisson
de son mystère
et le buisson vivait
dans la flamme
qui se posait sur lui
mourant sans fin
pour renaître en feu

Épiphanie de l'envoi
il reflétait le souffle
qui l'habitait
et ouvrirait le futur
dans un baptême
de nouvelle naissance

Le messager d'incandescence
en luit
resplendissait de compassion
illuminait le chemin de liberté
conduisant à la promesse
déjà le pays haletait son attente

Moïse écoutait
hésitait
résistait

image du peuple qu'il conduirait bientôt
du pays du murmure
aux rivages de l'abandon-confiance

Tout allait s'accomplir

THE NAME[20]

The Name
was burning the bush
of their mystery
and the bush lived
in the flame
which rested on it
endlessly dying
and reborn in fire

Epiphany of sending
it reflected the breath
who lived in it
and would open the future
in a baptism
of new birth

The incandescent messenger
in it[21]
was shining with compassion
illuminating the path of freedom
leading to the promise
already the country panted its wait

20. In a desert, God revealed themself to Moses through a burning bush
that was not consumed by the fire. There, the latter received his calling to be
the leader that will drive the Israelites out of Egypt, where they were slaves, to
go to the promised land.

21. There is a play in the original text impossible to translate in English: the pro-
noun 'it' in French has the same sound than the preterit of the verb 'glow', used here.

Moses was listening
hesitated
resisted
image of the people he would soon lead
from the land of murmurs
to the shores of surrender-trust

Everything was to be accomplished

PASSAGE

Pharaon et ses chars approchaient

L'affrontement viendrait venger le sang des premiers-nés
en leurs cœurs, la douleur retentissait comme un grand cri de guerre,
    inextinguible

Pharaon et ses chars approchaient

Le peuple des hébreux tremblait
devant lui la mer lui barrait le chemin de ses lèvres fermées
impossible à franchir
les esclaves libérés pourraient seul succomber
le combat n'aurait pas de pitié

Pharaon et ses chars approchaient

La frayeur s'abattait sur les fils d'Israël
le ricanement du crépuscule savourait déjà leur défaite
et les fauchait de peur
les ombres menaçantes s'allongeaient vers le camp
comme des messagers de mort

Pharaon, Pharaon et ses chars approchaient

Leur vie allait s'éteindre dans ces ténèbres enragées
la nuit tuerait l'avenir promis
jusqu'à le raser de toute aurore

Pharaon et ses chars, Pharaon et ses chars

L'angoisse grandissait, atteignant l'épouvante
l'épreuve n'était plus à la mesure de l'homme
leurs faces rejoignaient la poussière du sol
comme pour goûter déjà l'amertume de disparaître
de leurs yeux criait un seul gémissement
le désespoir

Pharaon et ses chars

Leurs cœurs n'étaient qu'un cri
harcelant de détresse
hurlant d'extrémité

Visage contre terre
Moïse priait
un clapotis impassible semblait seul lui répondre

Ils approchent

Moïse poursuivait
le clapotis continuait
indifférent

Ils approchent, ils approchent

Dans la sueur de sang de sa grande agonie
le peuple suppliait
il implorait encore

Moïse poursuivait
crucifié par sa foi dans l'invisible
le cœur transpercé d'espérance

Pharaon et ses chars
ils arrivent

Ils sont là

Alors
Moïse se releva de terre
levant sur les eaux impassible
lourdes comme pierre de tombeau
le bois de la victoire

<pre>
          et les flots   s'ouvrirent
        comme un gi-   ron de femme
          s'apprêtant   à enfanter
      son premier-né   dans un éclat de
    joie, et Israël com-   mença la longue
      traversée de son   histoire, témoin
    de la tendresse divi-   ne peuple-louange
  nation-prêtre de l'Al-   liance irrévocable
</pre>

Au soupir du matin
la nuit referma ses flots sur Pharaon
engloutissant l'armée dans ses flammes d'embrun

C'était le troisième jour après la Pâque

THE PASSING

Pharaoh and his chariots were approaching

The confrontation would come to avenge the blood of the firstborns
in their hearts, pain resounded like a great, inextinguishable battle
    cry

Pharaoh and his chariots were approaching

The Hebrew people trembled
in front of them, the sea barred the path with its closed lips
impossible to cross
the freed slaves could only succumb
the fight would have no mercy

Pharaoh and his chariots were approaching

Terror fell upon the children of Israel
the sneer of the twilight was already savoring their defeat
and mowing them down with fear
the threatening shadows were lengthening towards the camp
like messengers of death

Pharaoh, Pharaoh and his chariots were approaching

Their life was to be extinguished in raging darkness
the night would kill the promised future
until it was dawn-razed

Pharaoh and his chariots, Pharaoh and his chariots

The anguish grew, reaching terror
the ordeal was no longer commensurate with man
their gazes joined the dust of the ground
to already taste the bitterness of disappearing
from their eyes cried a single moan
despair

Pharaoh and his chariots

Their heart was but a cry
harassing in distress
screaming in extremity

Face down
Moses prayed
only an impassive lapping seemed to answer him

They are approaching

Moses pursued
the lapping continued
indifferent

They approach, they approach

In the bloody sweat of their great agony
the people pled
they begged again

Moses pursued
crucified by his faith in the unseen
his heart pierced with hope

Pharaoh and his chariots
they're coming

They're here

Then
Moses got up from the ground
raising on the waters unmoved
heavy as a tombstone
the wood of victory

                    and the waves   opened
                   like a woman's   bosom
                  getting ready to   give birth
                   to her firstborn   in a burst of
                  joy, and Israel   began the long
                 journey through its   history, witness
                of divine tenderness   people-praise
               nation-priest of the   irrevocable Covenant

At the sigh of the morning
the night closed its waves over Pharaoh
engulfing the army in its flames of sea spray

It was the third day after Passover

LA MONTAGNE

La montagne était en feu
transmuée
couronnée de divin

Moïse monta
enveloppé par le Souffle
aspiré par l'attente du ciel

Le sommet était comme coiffé de flammes

Et le doigt de l'alliance
écrivit les Paroles, les dix
sur la pierre
comme sur un cœur endurci
enclos
qu'elles tentaient d'ouvrir en grâce

De plus bas
vint un son
un veau
meugla

En haut de la montagne
le serviteur souffrant
qui serait
crucifié des péchés

pardonnant
supplierait

Et sa prière
comme un expir de tempête embrasée
démolirait toute séparation, tout mur
accomplissant l'extrême de la grâce
pour la transfigurer en
gloire

Le peuple du nouveau royaume
naîtrait

THE MOUNTAIN

The mountain was on fire
transmuted
crowned with divine

Moses went up
enveloped by the Breath
sucked in by the waiting of the sky

The summit was as if capped with flames

And the covenant finger
wrote the Words, the ten
on the stone
like on a hardened heart
enclosed
that they tried to open in grace

From bellow
a sound came
a calf
mooing

At the top
the suffering servant
who would be
crucified by sin

forgiving
would beg

And his prayer
like an exhale of a brazing storm
would tear down every separation, every wall
fulfilling the extreme of grace
to transfigure it into
glory

The new kingdom people
would be born

JOSUÉ

Le peuple avait passé le fleuve
dans un baptême de silence
l'arche en fête
inondant de vie les eaux de destruction
l'alliance stoppa la mort

Douze pierres, couronne de victoire
étaient à présent dressées sur la rive
elles criaient leur prière d'action-de-grâce
l'érigeant à jamais
dans la mémoire de Dieu

L'ange à l'épée de feu
avait déchiré la séparation
interdisant le pays promis

Plus loin
les murs de la cité
étaient tombés
dans un tremblement d'enfer

Sur la droite
le mont de bénédictions
se dressait
ouvrant au pécheur repenti le paradis
aujourd'hui

Sur la gauche
le mont de malédictions
que choisiras-tu?

Au centre
la Source sans fin
plongeait au cœur de Dieu-compassion
pour ressurgir
éternellement

Une femme en attente de mari
viendrait y puiser
la Vie

Et la nouvelle cité
belle comme une vision d'en-haut
surgirait bientôt
revêtue de
noces de feu

JOSHUA

The people had crossed the river
in a baptism of silence
the ark in celebration
flooding the waters of destruction with life
the covenant stopped death

Twelve stones, crown of victory
stood now on the shore
they shouted their prayer of thanksgiving
forever erecting it
in the memory of God

The angel with the flaming sword
had torn the separation
that banned the promised land

Further away
the city walls
had fallen
in a hellquake

On the right
the mount of blessings
was rising
opening Eden to the repentant sinner
today

On the left
the mount of curses
what will you choose?

In the center
the never-ending Source
was plunging into the heart of God-compassion
to reappear
eternally

A woman waiting for a husband
would draw from it
Life

And the new city
beautiful as a vision from above
would soon arise
dressed for
a marriage of fire

L'APPEL

Le respir des nuits
se mêlait à son âme

Ses mains sur le sol
écoutaient la pulsation paisible de l'envers
s'élevant en colonnes

Le temple du monde s'endormait
bercé par le murmure du temps
la fraîcheur de la lune pacifiait les ombres
loin des ardes[22] du jour

Le sourire des étoiles
l'enlaçait de lumière timide

Tout parlait l'Eternel

Il oubliait la souffrance en larmes
seule sa joie versait pleurs
et embrassait les anges
des caresses de son cœur
les séraphs l'étreignaient en retour
dans un souffle paresseux d'encens
rejoignant lentement le ciel

22. Forme poétique pour 'ardeurs'.

Les yeux clos
endormis
l'enfant s'élevait au-dessus des rêves
le cœur ouvert
prêt à l'à-venir

Quand
par deux fois
il entendit son nom

THE CALL[23]

The breath of the nights
mingled with his soul

His hands on the ground
listened to the peaceful pulsation of the reverse
rising in columns

The temple of the world fell asleep
lulled by the murmur of time
the coolness of the moon pacified the shadows
far from the blazes of the day

The smile of the stars
embraced him with shy light

Everything was telling the Eternal

He was forgetting any pain in tears
only his joy was crying
and kissing the angels
with caresses of his heart
the seraphs[24] hugged him back
in a lazy breath of incense
slowly reaching heaven

23. In the biblical story, Samuel was called by the Lord during the night, when he was a child serving in a temple.

24. Poetic form for 'Seraphims' (kind of angels), like in French.

With eyes closed
sleeping
the child was rising above the dreams
with an open heart
ready for the future

When
twice
he heard his name

L'ASCENSION

Le jour arriva

Les arbres vibraient de toutes feuilles, conduisant la cadence
Le soleil jouait de ses rayons dans les ailes d'oiseaux tourbillonnant
    de bonheur
Grisés de délices, les nuages dessinaient leur lente chorégraphie sur
    l'azur
Les champs se chamarraient de fleurs miroitant leurs couleurs
Des éclats de lumière papillonnaient de plaisir dans les ruisseaux
    parés de transparence

Tout riait d'allégresse
tout s'enivrait d'exultation
tout resplendissait d'une gaieté étincelante

Les tambourins battaient de toute force, enrythmés[25] par le son
    des cymbales
Les trompettes entrainaient les sistrums dans un ballet d'accords
Et les lyres et les flûtes envoutaient les harpes d'harmonies

David était là
vêtu comme un prêtre
virevoltant dans le souffle de la dance divine

Avec le bois devenu arche d'une alliance
il montait vers Jérusalem ornée telle une épouse

25. Néologisme.

Les gens le regardaient
interdit ou ravi
emporté ou en garde

Qu'importait-il
le jour était de joie
et la vie s'envolait vers son avenir
et la vie s'envolait vers
toi

THE ASCENSION

The day came

The trees were vibrating with all their leaves, driving the cadence
The sun was playing its rays in the wings of birds swirling with
    happiness
Filled with delight, the clouds were drawing their slow choreo-
    graphy on the azure
The fields were full of flowers shimmering in colour
Bursts of light were fluttering with elation in streams adorned with
    transparency

Everything was giggling with exultation
everything was drunk with jubilation
everything was dazzling with sparkling cheerfulness

Tambourines were beating with all their might, enlivened by the
    sound of cymbals
Trumpets brought sistrums into a chord ballet
Lyres and flutes spelled the harps with harmonies

David was there
dressed like a priest
twirling in the breath of the divine dance

With the wood turned ark of a covenant
he was ascending to Jerusalem adorned as a bride

The people were looking at him
astonished or delighted
enthusiastic or taken aback

Did it matter
it was a day of delight
and life was flying towards its future
and life was flying towards
you

LA CITHARE

Saül était assis, sa lance à la main, écoutant la Beauté

Et les doigts de David, comme des papillons, butinaient le nectar
des cordes soleil-argent ; et les mains de David se balançaient
ensemble comme des navires sur les flots de l'origine

Les notes s'échappaient ; le poète façonnait leur argile, potier du
Mystère, et la mélodie venait comme une ondée caresser le vis-
age du vieux roi fatigué

La cithare chantait sous l'amour du berger, ses doigts étaient ses
cordes et ses cordes riaient ; le cœur du pastoureau embras-
sait l'instrument et leurs chants se mêlaient, encens d'un soir
de lune

Au chant de leur union, la cithare grandissait comme un mât de
vaisseau dressé sur l'univers, une ancre de la terre soudée aux
flots du ciel, tandis que les paumes de David s'élevaient vers le
pré des étoiles perdues

Tout son être n'est plus que ce chant qui brûle dans ses veines, il
n'est plus que musique courant sur les flammes du temps

Et les bras de la cithare enlacèrent les siens pour, tendrement, sur
son sein, déposer le berger, réchauffant sa pâleur

David, en sa vie étendue sur le bois, s'offrait comme une hostie

Ta cithare, berger, n'a plus pour corde que ton corps épousant le
  chant qui résonne dans les notes du monde ; il vibre sans pa-
  roles dans un souffle invisible, grand cri fécondant la terre de
  ton Amour qui coule en sang

Et le chant de David éclot comme un printemps au midi de sa
  course pour se transfigurer en silence de vie qui germe ; la
  cithare empourprée l'étreignait sur son âme, pleurant

Dans le creux d'une joue, le vieux roi fatigué sentait couler une
  larme
elle murmurait l'attente d'une noce annoncée

THE ZITHER[26]

Saul was seated, spear in hand, listening to the beauty

And David's fingers, like butterflies, gathered nectar from the sun-silver strings; and David's hands were swinging together like ships on the original waves

The notes escaped; the poet shaped their clay, potter of the mystery, and the melody came like a shower to caress the face of the tired old king

The zither sang under the shepherd's love, his fingers were her strings, and her strings laughed; the heart of the shepherd kissed the instrument, and their songs mingled, incense of a moonlit evening

At the song of their union, the zither grew like a ship's mast erected on the universe, an anchor of the earth welded to the waves of the sky, while the palms of David rose towards the meadow of the lost stars

His whole being is nothing more than this song that burns in his veins, he is nothing more than music running on the flames of time

And the arms of the zither entwined his to tenderly place the shepherd on her bosom, warming his pallor

26. Although 'zither' is neutral in English, it is here personalized and become a 'she'.

David, in his life stretched out on the wood, offered himself as a host

Your zither, shepherd, no longer has a string except your body
   marrying the song that resounds in the notes of the world; it
   vibrates without words in an invisible breath, a great cry fertil-
   izing the earth with your Love flowing in blood

And David's song blossomed like a midday spring to be transfig-
   ured into the silence of life germinating; the crimson zither
   clutched him in her soul, weeping

In the hollow of a cheek
the tired old king felt a tear flow
it murmured the expectation of an announced wedding

EN-DOR

Et l'ombre du prophète monta des profondeurs

Saul frémit
l'air se figea
le temps palpitait de peur

L'effroi recouvrit l'espace
d'un invisible manteau de glace
étouffant tout souffle
comme un serpent

Le roi brisé attendait
à n'en pouvoir respirer
son front suintait la terreur

Et le vieil homme fut là
dressé devant lui
statue blanche aux lèvres vivantes

Les lèvres s'ouvrirent
tombeau qui recrachait son mort
pour le sentencier à nouveau

La condamnation
retentit
verdict impassible
écho résonnant
comme un silencieux crissement d'âme
en agonie

L'ordalie
torturait le désir-vivre
à le détruire

Et l'ombre disparut

Saul demeura

Un dernier jour

qui disparaîtrait
dans l'écarlate d'un glaive
dégoulinant de vie perdue

Il renaîtrait dans l'espérance offerte
d'un agneau
ouvrant la mort
à la tuer

ENDOR[27]

And the shadow of the prophet rose from the depths

Saul shuddered
the air froze
time palpitated with angst

Scare covered the space
with an invisible coat of ice
suffocating all breaths
like a snake

The broken king was waiting
unable to respire
his brow was oozing terror

And the old man was there
standing before him
white statue with living lips

The lips opened
tomb spitting its dead
to sentence it again

27. Endor is the place where king Saul, already rejected by God, sought to consult the prophet Samuel now dead, to win victory against the Philistine armies.

The conviction
rung out
impassive verdict
echo resonant
like a silent screeching of a soul
in agony

The ordeal
was torturing the desire-to-live
to the destruction

And the shadow was gone

Saul was remaining

One last day

that would disappear
in the scarlet of a sword
dripping with lost life

It would be reborn in the hope offered
of a lamb
opening death
to kill it

LE MONT GUILBOA

Les oiseaux entrelaçaient leurs vols
pour former une tapisserie de danses
flottant sur l'horizon
ils virevoltaient comme volutes d'encens du soir

Le soleil ruisselait sa lumière
éclaboussant de couleurs en feu
la toile des cieux
son éclat de vie se reflétait en farandole
dans les nuages devenus fournaises
et des dorures de braises s'enchevêtraient bientôt
avant de disparaître en étincellements de pastels

L'été se chamarrait de teintes polychromes
et le peintre du temps
déjà
préparait en secret de feuillage
la symphonie des automnes qui retentirait

Tout pétillait de plaisir
tout fredonnait de frissons clandestins
tout s'épanouissait en s'évanouissant

Dans les champs, au bas des vagues de collines
océan de pierre ondulant immobile
les épis se dressaient fièrement
comme gardiens de ces jours
déployant comme des étendards
leur chevelure dorée par une étoile

Sur le mont Guilboa
s'élançaient la vigueur des silhouettes d'arbre
revêtus de leur lustre

Au milieu des racines
encore jeunes
des cadavres entremêlaient leurs membres
le son rauque d'un râle, un dernier
lacéra l'espace devenu nuit

Puis ce fut le silence

MOUNT GILBOA [28]

Birds were intertwining their flights
to form a tapestry of dances
floating on the horizon
They were twirling like spirals of evening incense

The sun was flowing its light
splashing with colors on fire
the canvas of heaven
Its living brilliance was reflected in farandole
in the clouds turned furnaces
and gilds of embers were soon getting tangled
before disappearing into sparkling pastels

Summer was full of polychrome shades
and the painter of time
already
secretly prepared the foliage
to the autumn symphony that would resound

Everything was sparkling with pleasure
everything was whispering with a clandestine thrill
everything was blossoming as it was vanishing

28. The battle of Mount Gilboa saw the defeat of the armies of Israel, as well
as the death of King Saul and his son Jonathan, David's close friend.

In the fields, at the bottom of the waves of hills
ocean of stone undulating motionless
the ears were standing proudly
as guardians of these days
flying like flags
their hair golden by a star

On the mount Gilboa
the vigor of tree figures sprang
clad in their glory

Among the roots
still young
corpses were entwining their limbs
the hoarse sound of a rale, a last
lacerated the space turned night

Then there was only silence

LA MORT DU FILS

Le ciel s'était voilé de pudeur
la chaleur s'éteignait
bientôt le jour
s'enterrerait
dans l'horizon du crépuscule

David venait d'apprendre
et les mots le crucifiaient
comme un tocsin riant à mort

Un cri lui creusait l'âme
ainsi qu'un couteau vif
soudain il était rongé de vide

Et son cœur était éventré
comme l'orbite creuse
d'un œil gougé
qui ne refléterait plus vie
mais rien

Il était volé d'une présence
qui chantait l'avenir
le futur devenait poids
écrasant la nuit

Les chants de triomphe résonnaient autour

mais la victoire n'avait pour lui

qu'un goût de vinaigre

sur des plaies

une caresse

qui faisait frémir son être

d'horreur

Il la reconnaissait

c'était la louve

hurlant la mort

comme un destin

glué à son âme

qui trop souvent l'avait

rencontré

Dans sa douleur

il était seul

réduit à la corde

de son être

seulement père

Et son fils n'était

ni rebelle, ni ennemi

ou adversaire qui s'érigeait

il était seulement

son fils

son bien-aimé

qui plus n'était

qui plus n'était

Dans la mort du fils
pleurait celle du père

THE DEATH OF THE SON[29]

The sky had veiled in modesty
the heat was going out
soon the day
would bury itself
in the twilight horizon

David had just learned
and the words were crucifying him
like a tocsin laughing to death

A cry hollowed out his soul
like a sharp knife
suddenly he was consumed with emptiness

And his heart was ripped open
like a hollow socket
of a gouged eye
that no longer would reflect life
but nothing

He was robbed of a presence
who sang the future
the forthcoming was becoming a weight
crushing the night

29. Absalom, one of the sons of King David, rebelled against him and usurped power, driving his father out of Jerusalem. He died in a battle against the factions remaining loyal to David, who collapsed on hearing of his son's death.

Songs of triumph were echoing around
but the victory had for him
only a taste of vinegar
on wounds
a caress
that made his being shudder
with horror

He recognized her
it was the she-wolf
howling to death
like a destiny
glued to his soul
who too often had him
encountered

In his pain
he was alone
reduced to the rope
of his being
only father

And his son was not
neither rebel nor enemy
adversary who stood up
he was only
his son
his beloved

who no longer was

who no longer was

In the death of the son
cried that of the father

L'INVASION

Dieu ne les sauverait pas
Jérusalem tomberait de son haut
comme d'autres avant elle
à présent drapées de cris en sang
leur arrogance était maintenant muette
enterrée de terreur dans un tonnerre de flèches

L'assyrien se dressait de certitude
claquant ses mots comme une cravache
décharnant méthodiquement un dos d'esclave
Ezéchias, déjà vieilli
se courbait d'imploration

« Où étaient les dieux d'autrefois
qui protégeaient leurs villes?
Gisant impassibles
dans des poussières de prières sans répondre
Où serait le dieu d'Israël
devant la grandeur de l'empire en arme? »

Les paroles fracassaient l'âme
comme un bélier triomphant
Ezéchias regardait
les tentes étaient sans nombre
La Cité de Paix était encerclée de rires railleurs
qui écharpaient un silence de frayeur
Pour les combattre n'était
qu'un murmure étouffé de prophète

La nuit s'approchait comme une bête
et les vautours s'apprêtaient au festin promis

L'ombre recouvrit tout d'un linceul
couleur ténèbres

Au matin
il ne restait rien de l'armée de l'empire
qui fuyait Dieu

INVASION [30]

God wouldn't save them
Jerusalem would fall from her height
like others before her
now draped in blood cries
their arrogance was at once silenced
buried in terror in a thunder of arrows

The Assyrian was standing up with certainty
slamming his words like a whip
methodically fleshing out a slave's back
Hezekiah, already old
was bowing down with imploration

"Where were the gods of old
who protected their cities?
Lying impassive
in the dust of prayers without answering
Where would be the god of Israel
before the greatness of the empire in arms?"

30. The Neo-Assyrian king Sennacherib is known for having considerably expanded the extent of his empire. In particular, he destroyed the Northern Kingdom in Israel, and almost the entire Southern Kingdom, with Jerusalem and King Hezekiah surrounded and ready to fall. Only the prophet Isaiah was of a different opinion.

The words were shattering the soul
like a triumphant ram
Hezekiah looked
the tents were without number
The City of Peace was surrounded by mocking laughter
that was tearing up a silence of fear
To fight them was only
the stifled murmur of a prophet

Night was approaching like a beast
and the vultures were preparing for the promised feast

The shadow covered everything with a shroud
color of darkness

In the morning
nothing was left of the imperial army
that was flying from God

CRISE

Dans la pénombre de sa prison
Jérémie était assis

La même eau qui coulait du ciel
s'écoulait de ses yeux
gouttelettes de tristesse
s'engloutissant sous terre

L'amertume du non-sens
ruisselait au long de ses rides
et son regard s'éteignait de vie

Il était devenu un muet de mort
prophète qui n'ouvrait sa bouche
que pour maudire la terre au nom du ciel
et lui-même les cieux

Ses mots s'étaient mués en cris de poignard
qui frappaient l'âme en son cœur-être
il souffrait à s'en tordre
de la souffrance qu'il engendrait
et ne naîtrait qu'en dérision de lui

Chaque parole était à présent
un étouffement qui s'époumonait à se contenir
et chaque silence un brasier de destruction
où il se débattait de détresse
se noyant en son feu

Le combat atteignait sa limite
pour l'abattre
il semblait sans limite

Jérémie cherchait à oublier l'appel
mais le Verbe l'embrasait encore plus au profond
les sons s'entrechoquaient en lui
comme un tocsin enfiévré
qui s'engouffrait entre ses lèvres
brisant toute digue

Et la voix retentit dans le souffle d'un murmure

« Si tu reviens
déjà là je suis »

CRISIS[31]

In the darkness of his prison
Jeremiah was sitting

The same water that was flowing from the sky
was flowing from his eyes
droplets of sadness
sinking underground

The bitterness of nonsense
was streaming along his wrinkles
and his gaze was extinguishing with life

He had become a mute of death
prophet who never opened his mouth
that to curse the earth in the name of heaven
and he himself the heavens

His words turned into dagger cries
that struck the soul in its core
And he was suffering to warp
of the suffering he generated
and would only be born in derision of him

---

31. Various passages in the book of Jeremiah show the prophet struggling
with a profound crisis of vocation.

Every word was now
a suffocation that was screaming in him to contain itself
And every silence a blaze of destruction
where he struggled with distress
drowning in its fire

The fight was reaching its limit
to knock it down
it seemed limitless

Jeremiah was trying to forget the call
but the Word was setting him ablaze still deeper
Sounds clashed within him
like a fevered tocsin
that would run between his lips
breaking any dam

And the voice sounded in the breath of a murmur

"If you come back
already there I am"

L'ATTENTE

Les murs étaient détruits
le temple n'était plus
l'arche avait disparue

L'espérance du peuple était
une armée d'ossements desséchés
gisant
sans vie
dans le val de l'obscur
un vautour veillait à ce que rien ne reste
l'œuf de la mort avait éclos

La promesse des étoiles
n'était plus désormais que la lueur d'un gémissement
répété toute la nuit
toutes les nuits

Il faisait froid dans les entrailles

Mais près du fleuve
un char illuminé d'yeux béants de lumière
proclamait déjà le retour

Et le souffle des quatre vents
brûlait déjà de vie
les corps encore éteints
la promesse scintillait
gravée sur un cœur d'homme

L'alliance serait renouvelée
l'alliance serait nouvelle

THE WAIT

The walls were destroyed
the temple was no more
the ark had disappeared

The hope of the people was
an army of dry bones
lying
without life
in the valley of darkness
a vulture was watching so that nothing remained
the egg of death had hatched

The promise of the stars
was now only the glimmer of a moan
repeated all night
every night

It was cold in the guts

But near the river
a chariot illuminated with gaping eyes of light
already proclaimed the return

And the breath of the four winds
was already burning with life
the still dead bodies
the promise sparkled
engraved on a human heart

The covenant would be renewed
the covenant would be new

www.ingramcontent.com/pod-product-compliance
Lightning Source LLC
Chambersburg PA
CBHW070740030726
47601CB00001B/82